PRIMARY PARTNERS

A- Z Activities
to Make Learning Fun

for Ages 4-7
(CHOOSE THE RIGHT A)

Fun-to-Make Visuals ◻ Copy-and-Create Crafts

Simple Supplies Needed ◻ Matching Thought Treats

USE FOR PRIMARY LESSONS AND FAMILY HOME EVENING
to Reinforce Gospel Topics

You'll Find: A-Z Topics to Match Primary Lessons

Atonement   Baptism   Birth of Jesus   Blessings   Child of God
Choose The Right   Church   Christmas   Easter   Example   Families
Forgiveness   Follow Jesus   Gratitude   Happiness   Holy Ghost
Jesus   Kindness   Laws   Love   Missionary   Obedience
Peacemaker   Prayer   Priesthood Blessings   Reverence   Sabbath
Sacrament   Second Coming   Service   Sharing   Talents
Teaching Treasures   Temptations   Thank You   Tithing   Truth

97 98 99 00 01   10 9 8 7 6 5 4 3 2

Primary Partners: Ages 4-7, Choose the Right-A

Covenant Communications, Inc.
ISBN 1-55503-905-7

INTRODUCTION

PRIMARY PARTNERS
A-Z Activities to Make Learning Fun
for Choose The Right A   Ages 4-7

Children and parents alike will love the easy, fun-to-create visuals contained in this volume. Patterns for each of the projects are actual size, ready to Copy-n-Create in minutes. You'll enjoy using many of the Primary Partners crafts and activities to supplement the Primary 2* lessons, enhance your family home evenings, and help children learn gospel principles in fun, creative ways.

HOW TO USE THIS BOOK

1. **Preview A-Z Table of Contents** to find pictures and subjects.
2. **Use Lesson Cross Reference Index** on page iv. Match your lesson number with the A-Z subject to find activities quickly.
3. **Shop Ahead For Simple Supplies.** Each activity requires a few basic items: Copies of patterns, scissors, tape, glue, crayons, zip-close plastic bags, lunch size sacks, boxes, paper punch, yarn or ribbon, string, wooden craft sticks, metal brads, and safety pins.
4. **Copy Patterns Ahead.** You'll save time and avoid last-minute preparation.
5. **Organize Activities** in an A-Z file. Copy instructions to include with the pattern copies and supplies.

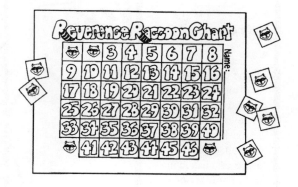

6. **Reward for Reverence.** Copy a Reverence Raccoon Chart and raccoon glue-on stickers on pages 80-81 for each child. When children are reverent during the lesson reward them with a raccoon they can glue on their chart (weeks #1-46). If they are not as reverent as they should be, don't give them a raccoon, (or cut a raccoon in half). Next week when they see their chart they are reminded of what they need to do to earn a Reverence Raccoon reward.
See Reverence lesson # 21 (pages 60-62) featuring the Reverence Raccoon cap.
7. **Create a Testimony Treasure Box** to store classroom creations.

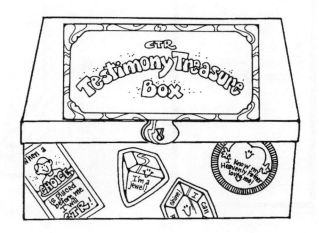

You'll Need: Copy of CTR Treasure Box label, glue-on stickers, and "Dear Parents" note (pages ii and iii), and a shoe or shirt box for each child, scissors, glue, contact paper, and crayons. **TO MAKE BOX:**
Step #1: Cover box with contact paper.
Step #2: Color and cut out label and glue-on stickers.
Step #3: Glue label and stickers on box.
Step #4: Send home the "Dear Parents" note (glue on inside lid or tape on top).

*Primary 2-CTR A manual is published by The Church of Jesus Christ of Latter-day Saints, Salt Lake City, Utah.

TO SUPPLEMENT THIS TREASURE BOX ACTIVITY:
Create a Heavenly Treasures activity from the book SUPER SCRIPTURE ACTIVITIES: I'm Trying to Be Like Jesus (see back page for details).

You'll find more glue-on stickers for the CTR Testimony Treasure Box and a show-and-tell presentation telling children to choose treasures that are of lasting worth.

Dear Parents:
This is

_____'s

CTR Testimony Treasure Box

Each week, please encourage your child to display the activity creations made in Primary or family home evening.
Self-esteem builds as visuals are shown and lessons retold. Plus, they help reinforce gospel learning.
Then, store testimony treasures in this, their very own CTR Testimony Treasure Box.

Thank you.

_____
Primary Teacher

PATTERN: CTR Testimony Treasure Box pocket to glue on top of activity storage box with "Dear Parents" note (below)

LESSON CROSS REFERENCE INDEX to Primary 2-CTR A manual*

*Primary 2-CTR A manual is published by the Church of Jesus Christ of Latter-day Saints, Salt Lake City, Utah.

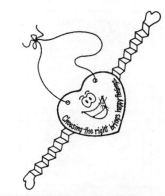

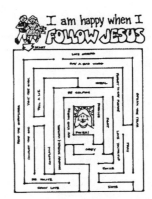

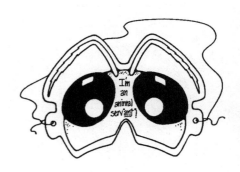

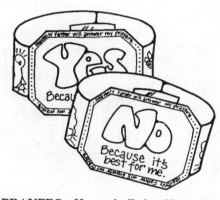

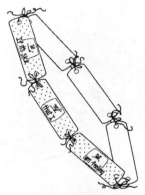

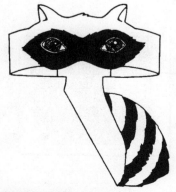

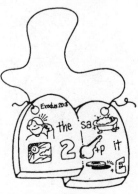

ATONEMENT: I Can Be Resurrected Like Jesus

(All Eyes Can See resurrection glasses)

See lesson #41 in Primary 2-CTR A manual*.

YOU'LL NEED: Copy of resurrection glasses (page 2) on colored cardstock paper for each child, scissors, glue or tape, and crayons

ACTIVITY: Remind children that because Jesus was resurrected, all can be resurrected again. Even the blind will be able to see again. Wear these resurrection glasses to remind you of this miracle.
1. Color and cut out resurrection glasses.
2. Glue or tape sides onto glasses to fit child's face.

THOUGHT TREAT: <u>Fresh Fruit or Vegetables</u>. Tell children that after the resurrection, we will have our bodies again and can eat these healthy snacks Heavenly Father has created for us.

BAPTISM: I'm Trying to Be Like Jesus

(two-sided baptism puzzle)

See lesson #12 in Primary 2-CTR A manual*.

I want to be baptized!

YOU'LL NEED: Copy of two-sided baptism puzzle (page 3) on colored cardstock paper, an envelope or zip-close plastic sandwich bag to store puzzle pieces for each child, scissors, glue, and crayons

ACTIVITY: Remind children to follow Jesus and be baptized. Create a two-sided baptism puzzle with Jesus and John on one side and children on the other.
1. Color pictures.
2. Cut around outside edge of puzzle first (don't cut puzzle pieces yet).
3. Fold pictures in half on dividing line back-to-back.
4. Glue pictures together (spreading glue over the entire piece, not just the edges).
5. Cut puzzle shapes out as shown on one side (six pieces).
6. Place puzzle in an envelope or plastic bag for each child to take home.

THOUGHT TREAT: <u>Footprint Cookies</u>. Roll sugar cookie dough into two-inch balls. Make imprint in dough with side of fist. Then press down with fingers at the top to make toes. <u>To Color Toenails</u>: Mix food coloring with sugar in bottle and shake well. Sprinkle on toes, or mix one teaspoon canned milk with food coloring and paint toes. Bake 350° for 8-10 minutes.

I'm trying to be like Jesus.

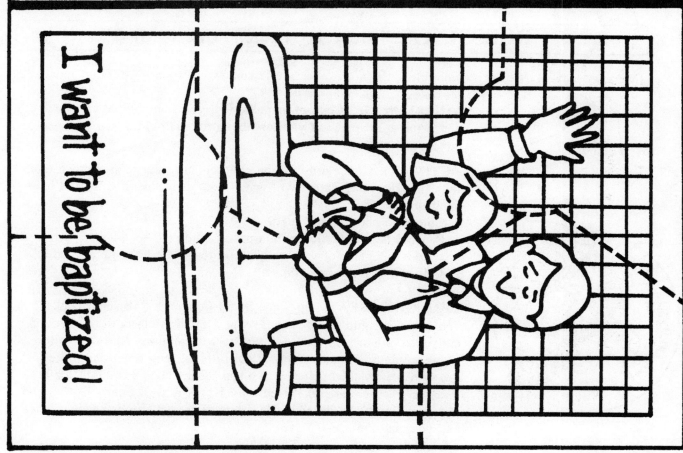

I want to be baptized!

BIRTH OF JESUS Brings Joy to the World

(dual shepherd and angel headband)

See lesson #7 in Primary 2-CTR A manual*.

YOU'LL NEED: Copy of dual shepherd and angel headband (pages 5-6) on colored cardstock paper for each child, scissors, glue, and crayons

ACTIVITY: Create a dual-sided shepherd and angel headband for role-play.
1. Color headband.
2. Glue or tape together.
TO ROLE-PLAY:
1. To role-play the shepherds when they are looking for Jesus, turn sheep side forward and say: "I am a shepherd. I found the baby Jesus."
2. To role-play the angel pointing the way to Jesus, turn star side forward and say: "I am an angel. I told the shepherds where to find the baby Jesus."

THOUGHT TREAT: Baby Jesus Birthday Cake. Sing a happy birthday song, adding the name "Jesus" as you sing. Pretend to blow out an invisible candle.

BLESSINGS: Heavenly Father Protects Me

(Me and Heavenly Father medallion)

See lesson #8 in Primary 2-CTR A manual*.

YOU'LL NEED: Copy of medallion (page 7) on colored cardstock paper and a 26" piece of yarn or ribbon for each child, scissors, paper punch, and crayons

ACTIVITY: Create a medallion children can wear to strengthen their faith that Heavenly Father will watch over them, bless them, and help them in time of need.
1. Color and cut out medallion.
2. Punch a hole at the top with a paper punch.
3. Lace a 26" piece of yarn or ribbon through the hole, tie at the top, and place medallion on child.

THOUGHT TREAT: Sunshine Sugar Cookies: Roll sugar cookie dough and cut into round shapes. Cut a small circle in the center and cut sun rays half way into each cookie with a knife. Sprinkle yellow sugar on top. To make yellow sugar, mix 1/2 cup sugar and a few drops of yellow food coloring in a bag. Bake cookies at 350° for 8-10 minutes. Tell children that Heavenly Father is your Sunny Day Friend and your Rainy Day Friend. He wants to hear about your happy times and your sad times.

   *Primary 2-CTR A manual is published by The Church of Jesus Christ of Latter-day Saints, Salt Lake City, Utah.

I am an angel. I told the shepherds where to find baby Jesus.

I am a shepherd, I found the baby Jesus.

GLUE TO SIDE A

ADJUST FOR SIZE & GLUE TO SIDE C

GLUE TO SIDE B

CHILD OF GOD: We Are All Heavenly Father's Children

(heavenly family photo and frame)

See lesson #3 in Primary 2-CTR A manual*.

YOU'LL NEED: Copy of heavenly family photo (page 9) on colored cardstock paper and 12" string or ribbon for each child, an egg carton, scissors, glue, and crayons

ACTIVITY: Help each child put him or herself in a portrait with Heavenly Father and Jesus and other children to know they are part of a heavenly family.
1. Color and cut out photo and girl or boy.
2. Cut out three small 1/4" squares of egg carton and glue on silhouette squares.
3. Glue girl or boy on silhouette image on photo (over egg carton squares--so image will stand out).
4. Fold frame according to directions and glue corner.
5. Tape string to the back of framed photo to hang on the wall.

THOUGHT TREAT:
Gingerbread Girl or Boy Cookie.
Remind children that they are created in the image of Heavenly Father and Jesus.

CHOOSING THE RIGHT Brings Happy Feelings

(happy heart medallion)

See lesson #26 in Primary 2-CTR A manual*.

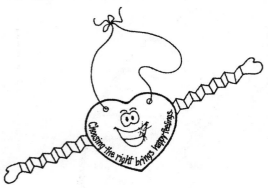

YOU'LL NEED: Copy of happy heart medallion, arm and hand (page 10) on red cardstock paper and 26" yarn or ribbon for each child, scissors, glue, paper punch, and crayons

ACTIVITY: Create a happy heart medallion with accordion arms to remind each child that "Choosing the right brings happy feelings."

OPTION #1: If copied on cardstock paper cut arms in half and use only one heart, face, and set of hands (following directions below).
OPTION #2: If copied on lightweight paper:
1. Color and cut out medallion, arms and hands.
2. Fold arms in half and glue inside.
3. Fold hands back at wrist and glue part "B" of hand to part "B" of arm (gluing hands together).
4. Fan fold arms.
5. Glue heart face back to back, gluing arms inside face with thumbs up.
6. Paper punch top left and right of heart.
7. Tie ends of yarn or ribbon through each hole, and place around child's neck.

THOUGHT TREAT: Cherry Cheery Smile Cookies.
Add finely chopped maraschino cherries to sugar cookie dough (with 1/4 cup extra flour). Roll out dough and cut into heart shapes. Bake at 350° for 8-10 minutes. Tell children that this cherry cookie is to remind them to be sure and wear a cheery or happy smile to show others that you want to choose the right.

*Primary 2-CTR A manual is published by The Church of Jesus Christ of Latter-day Saints, Salt Lake City, Utah.

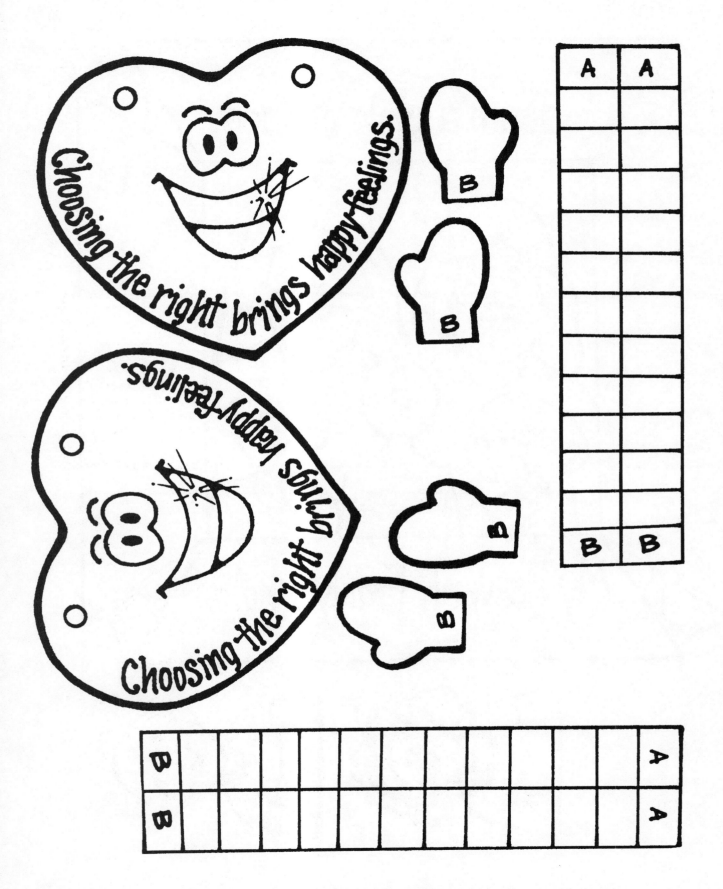

Choosing the right brings happy feelings.

Choosing the right brings happy feelings.

*Primary 2-CTR A manual is published by The Church of Jesus Christ of Latter-day Saints, Salt Lake City, Utah.

CHOOSE THE RIGHT: Heavenly Father Gave Me Free Agency

(choices slap game)

See lesson #5 in Primary 2-CTR A manual*.

YOU'LL NEED: Copy of slap pad (page 12) and game rules (below) and crayons for each child

ACTIVITY: Help the child make choices by slapping the frowning faces or the smiling faces slap pad when a choice is given them.
1. Color frown and smile slap pads and place in front of each child.
2. Read the choices (following game rules).
3. Staple rules to slap pad for child to take home.

THOUGHT TREAT: Smiling Face Cookies. Decorate sugar cookie with frosting and create a mile with contrasting colored frosting.

CHOOSE THE RIGHT Choices Slap Game Rules:
Slap frown with left hand if the choice is wrong. Slap smile with right hand if choice is right.

♥ I come to Primary. ♥ I thank my teacher. ♥ I poke my friend instead of folding my arms. ♥ I sing when asked to sing in Primary. ♥ I say excuse me. ♥ I keep my eyes open when the prayer is said. ♥ I bring a friend to Primary. ♥ I yell in the chapel. ♥ I whisper to my friend during the sacrament. ♥ I push a friend away from the fountain. ♥ I walk quietly going to my classroom. ♥ I wait for my turn to have a treat. ♥ I laugh when another child falls down. ♥ I raise my hand in class before talking. ♥ I make noises during class. ♥ I sing with my best voice. ♥ I help the teacher with an activity. ♥ I fold my arms. ♥ I laugh and make fun of someone in class. ♥ I say please when I need help. ♥ I listen quietly when my teacher tells a story. ♥ I choose the right.

CHOOSE THE RIGHT: I Can Make Choices

(choose-and-match puzzle)

See lesson #2 in Primary 2-CTR A manual*.

YOU'LL NEED: Copy of match puzzle (page 13) on colored cardstock paper, zip-close plastic bag for each child, scissors, and crayons

ACTIVITY: Help children match cards to the center card that reads: "THINK: What Would Jesus Want Me to Do?" **To Match Puzzle:** Place card symbols next to the symbols that match, i.e. dots with dots and hearts with hearts. From there they can match the right action, i.e. the "Make" card with the "Bed" card.
1. Color and cut out puzzle patterns.
2. Match action cards as detailed above.
3. Place puzzle pieces in a plastic zip-close bag for each child to take home.

THOUGHT TREAT: CTR Cookies. Decorate sugar cookie with frosting and write CTR with contrasting colored frosting.

CHOOSE THE RIGHT: I Will Be Wise and Follow Jesus

(wise man, foolish man flip-flag)

See lesson #36 in Primary 2-CTR A manual*.

YOU'LL NEED: Copy of flip-flag (page 15) on colored cardstock paper, and a wooden craft stick (or unsharpened pencil) for each child, scissors, glue, and crayons

ACTIVITY: Create a wise man and foolish man flip-flag to remind children that they are wise when they follow Jesus. To flip the flag, move it fast left and right to try and see both sides at once. Remind them that when they have two choices to make, they should slow down and pray about their choices. Then they can choose the right.
1. Color and cut out flag.
2. Glue a wooden stick in the bottom center.
3. Fold and glue back to back.

THOUGHT TREAT: Smiling House Sugar Cookies. Use pattern on page 16 to cut out sugar cookie dough in house shape. Decorate house with a smile like the wise man's house. Remind children that as they choose the right, they put a smile on everyone's face.

CHURCH: The Church of Jesus Christ is on the Earth Again

(Then and Now sticker fun poster)

See lesson #42 in Primary 2-CTR A manual*.

YOU'LL NEED: Copy of sticker poster and glue-on stickers (pages 17-18) on colored cardstock paper for each child, scissors, glue, and crayons

ACTIVITY: Create a sticker poster with glue-on stickers to show The Church of Jesus Christ when Jesus was on the earth, and now when it has been restored to the earth again. Glue-on stickers show pictures of then and now.
1. Color and cut out glue-on stickers.
2. Glue stickers on the Then and Now boxes.

THOUGHT TREAT: Church House Cookies. Use pattern on page 16 to cut out sugar cookie dough in house shape. Decorate with frosting showing stick figures (people) sitting inside.

PATTERN: CHOOSE THE RIGHT (flip flag) See lesson #36 in Primary 2-CTR A manual*.

PATTERN: CHOOSE THE RIGHT (church cookie cutter)   See lesson #36 in Primary 2-CTR A manual*.

        *Primary 2-CTR A manual is published by The Church of Jesus Christ of Latter-day Saints, Salt Lake City, Utah.

The Church of Jesus Christ is on the earth again!

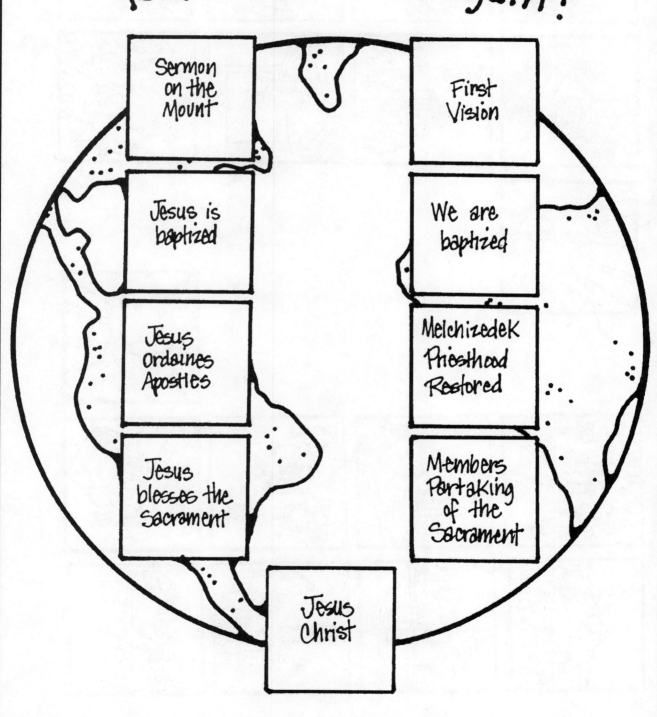

Sermon on the Mount

First Vision

Jesus is baptized

We are baptized

Jesus Ordaines Apostles

Melchizedek Priesthood Restored

Jesus blesses the Sacrament

Members Portaking of the Sacrament

Jesus Christ

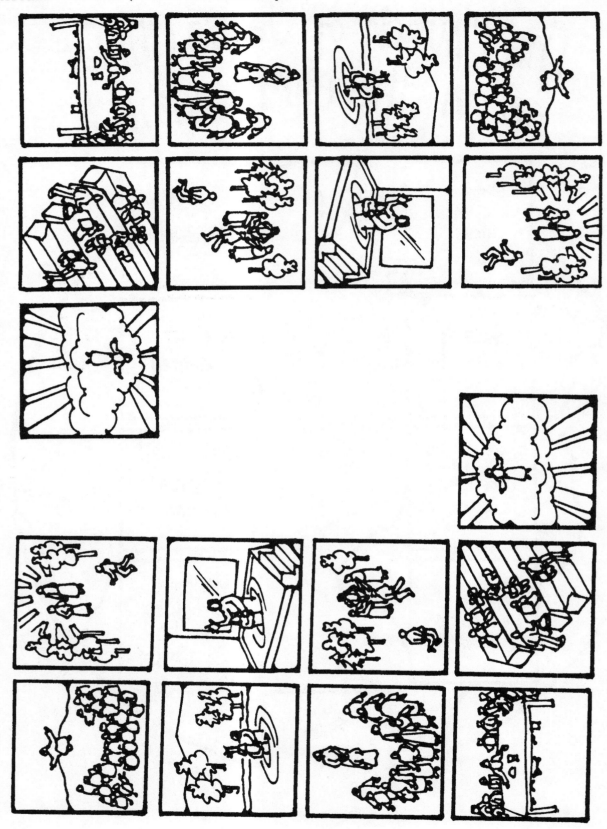

CHRISTMAS: Jesus Is Our Greatest Gift

(baby Jesus ornament)

See lesson #46 in Primary 2-CTR A manual*.

YOU'LL NEED: Copy of baby Jesus ornament pattern (page 20) on colored cardstock paper, 12" piece of yarn or ribbon for each child, scissors, (Option: contact paper to laminate), and crayons

ACTIVITY: Create an ornament each child can proudly hang on their Christmas tree or on their wall to remind them that "Jesus Is Our Greatest Gift."
1. Color and cut out ornament (OPTION: Before cutting, laminate with contact paper).
2. Fold down tabs and all box sides.
3. Fold baby Jesus center and place inside.
4. Glue side tabs inside box.
5. Fold and glue bow zig-zag line to box zig-zag line.
6. Poke a hole above bow with a pencil and thread a 12" string through to hang on tree.

THOUGHT TREAT: Gift Wrapped Treats. Tell children that the gift inside is sweet, but the sweetest gift of all is the gift Heavenly Father gave us when he sent his Son Jesus Christ to the earth.

EASTER: I Can Be Resurrected Like Jesus

(Easter morning match game)

See lesson #45 in Primary 2-CTR A manual*.

YOU'LL NEED: Copy two sets of match cards (page 21) on colored cardstock paper and zip-close plastic bag for each child, scissors, and crayons

ACTIVITY: Play an Easter morning match game to remind children that we celebrate Easter because Jesus was resurrected.
TO MAKE: Color and cut out match cards. Place extra sets in bag for children to take home.
TO PLAY: Turn two sets of match cards face down on table or floor. Children take turns turning two cards over to make a match. Turn them face down again if a match is not made. Each child who makes a match collects matched cards to win.

THOUGHT TREAT: Easter Egg Hunt. Remind children that we like to search for eggs because we are reminded of baby animals who are born in the spring. It is a new beginning for them. Easter is a new beginning for us. After we die and are resurrected, we get a new body.

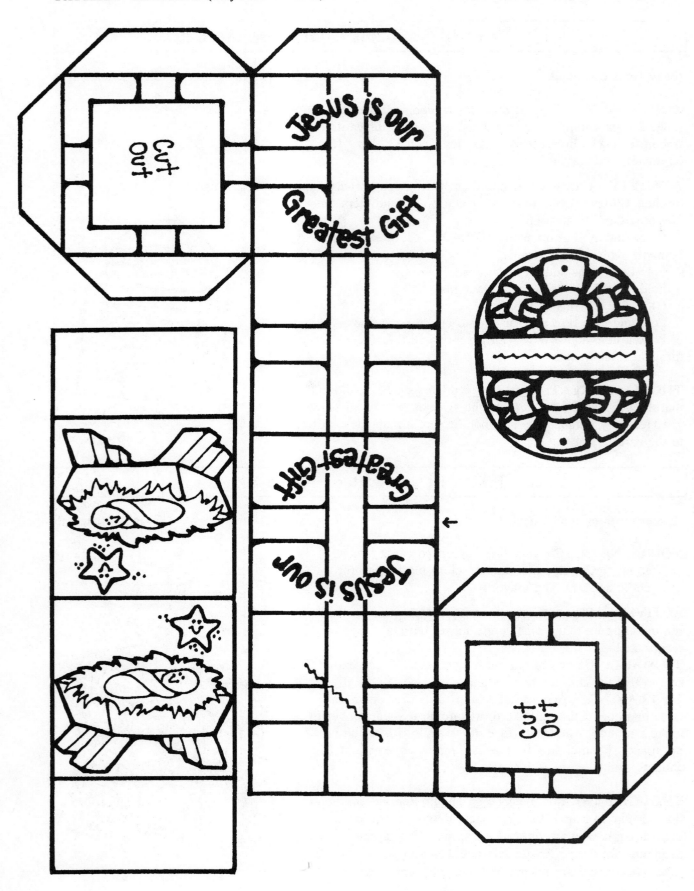

　　　*Primary 2-CTR A manual is published by The Church of Jesus Christ of Latter-day Saints, Salt Lake City, Utah.

EXAMPLE: I Can Be Like Jesus

(scripture scroll - Luke 2:52)

See lesson #9 in Primary 2-CTR A manual*.

YOU'LL NEED: Copy of scripture scroll (page 23) on colored lightweight paper and two wooden craft sticks for each child, scissors, glue, and crayons

ACTIVITY: Create a scripture scroll to help child learn how "Jesus increased in wisdom and stature, and in favour with God and man (Luke 2:52)."
1. Glue a wooden craft stick to each side ahead of time to allow to dry.
2. Color and cut out scroll.
3. Roll scroll around stick, rolling both ends to the middle with the scripture message inside.
4. Show children how to roll out the scroll and read the message. Tell them that in Jesus' day the leaders had scrolls, and many important messages were written on these scrolls. This message is important to show us that we too can be like Jesus (read scripture scroll).

THOUGHT TREAT: <u>Graham Crackers</u>. Serve one graham cracker with four parts to each child and talk about the four ways Jesus grew.

EXAMPLE: I Will Let My Light Shine

(church, school, home EXAMPLE candle mobile)

See lesson #29 in Primary 2-CTR A manual*.

YOU'LL NEED: Copy of candle mobile (page 24) on colored cardstock paper and 16" string for each child, scissors, glue, tape, and crayons

ACTIVITY: Create an EXAMPLE candle mobile with church, school, and home sides to hang in the home. Candle mobile can remind each child to let their light shine and be an example as Jesus taught (Matthew 5:14-16).
1. Color and cut out mobile.
2. Fold candle mobile and tape a 16" string half way down on inside.
3. Glue tabs.

THOUGHT TREAT: <u>Candle Cake</u>. Cupcake with a candle. Don't light in church--OK to light at home with adult supervision. Tell children when they choose the right they are being a good example, showing others how to act. When they choose the right, their light shines.

*Primary 2-CTR A manual is published by The Church of Jesus Christ of Latter-day Saints, Salt Lake City, Utah.

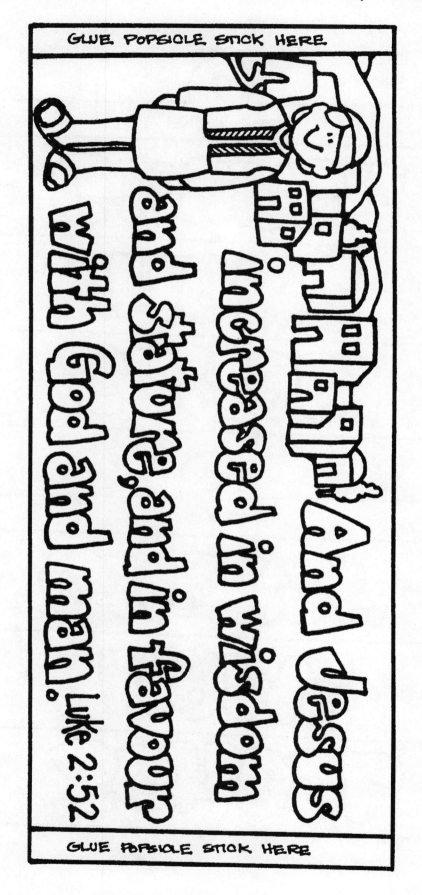

   *Primary 2-CTR A manual is published by The Church of Jesus Christ of Latter-day Saints, Salt Lake City, Utah.

FAMILIES Are Special

(missing family puzzle)

See lesson #6 in Primary 2-CTR A manual*.

YOU'LL NEED: Copy of puzzle (page 26) on colored cardstock paper and a zip-close plastic bag for each child, scissors, and crayons

ACTIVITY: Create a puzzle that includes each family member and help children know that Heavenly Father planned for us to grow up in families to love and help us.
1. Color and cut out puzzle.
2. Put puzzle together and talk about what it would be like if one person in this family were missing (taking that one person out of the puzzle).
3. Store each child's missing family puzzle pieces in a zip-close plastic bag.

THOUGHT TREAT: <u>Happy Family Face Pancakes</u>.
Pancakes decorated with blue pancake eyes and pink mouth.
1. Measure 1/4 cup of pancake batter into two different cups.
2. Mix a few drops of <u>blue</u> food coloring in 1/4 cup batter, and <u>red</u> food coloring in the second 1/4 cup of batter.
3. In a buttered frying pan make round pancakes as usual, adding two ears.
4. After frying pancake on one side, turn over.
5. Pour red pancake batter on cooked side of pancake to form a mouth, and blue batter to form eyes.
6. Turn pancake over and cook about 30 seconds.
Talk about how happy we are when our family is together.

FORGIVENESS: I Am Happy When I Forgive

(forgiving faces)

See lesson #40 in Primary 2-CTR A manual*.

YOU'LL NEED: Copy of forgiving faces (pages 27-28) on colored cardstock paper for each child, scissors, glue, and crayons

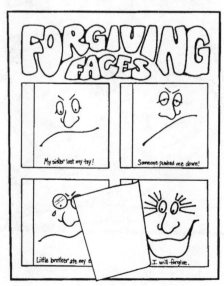

ACTIVITY: Enjoy opening the situation doors to discover forgiving faces. Help children understand they can be happy when they forgive.
1. Color and cut out situation doors and forgiving faces picture poster.
2. Glue situation doors over forgiving faces #1-4.
3. Help children open doors to look and talk about the situations and forgiving face responses.

THOUGHT TREAT: <u>Funny Face Cookies</u>. Round cookies decorated with frosting faces or dried fruit faces baked into cookie. Tell children that a face can tell us many things. It can tell how a person is feeling and forgiving.

PATTERN: FAMILIES (missing family puzzle)   See lesson #6 in Primary 2-CTR A manual*.

*Primary 2-CTR A manual is published by The Church of Jesus Christ of Latter-day Saints, Salt Lake City, Utah.

FORGIVING FACES

Glue bad face #1 here.

I will forgive.

Glue bad face #2 here.

I will forgive.

Glue bad face #3 here.

I will forgive.

Glue bad face #4 here.

I will forgive.

PATTERN: FORGIVENESS (forgiving faces)   See lesson #40 in Primary 2-CTR A manual*.

 *Primary 2-CTR A manual is published by The Church of Jesus Christ of Latter-day Saints, Salt Lake City, Utah.

FOLLOW JESUS: Before Earth Life I Choose to Follow Jesus

(pre-mortal life puppet show)

See lesson #4 in Primary 2-CTR A manual*.

YOU'LL NEED: Copy of pre-mortal life scene and puppets (pages 30-31) on colored cardstock paper, four wooden sticks or 4" straws (cut an 8" straw in half), and zip-close bag for each child, scissors, glue or tape, and crayons

ACTIVITY: Create a pre-mortal life puppet show. Then role-play pre-mortal life where we lived with Heavenly Father and Jesus.
1. Color and cut out puppets.
2. Glue-mount puppets on wooden sticks or tape to short straws.
3. Role-play, moving puppets across the pre-mortal life scene to show that we chose to follow Jesus.
4. Store puppet show in zip-close bag.

THOUGHT TREAT: Healthy Snacks (apple slices, carrot and celery sticks, raisins). Remind children that since we chose to come to earth and receive a body, we need to eat good foods to keep our body healthy and strong.

FOLLOW JESUS: I Will Choose the Right

(I Am Happy when I Follow Jesus decision maze)

See lesson #15 in Primary 2-CTR A manual*.

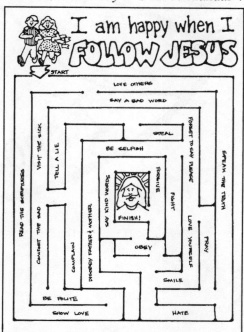

YOU'LL NEED: Copy of decision maze (page 32) on colored cardstock paper for each child, scissors, pencil, and crayons

ACTIVITY: Help children learn how to choose the right and follow Jesus, guiding them through the maze.
1. START at the beginning and guiding them past the wrong choices.
2. Pencil or color in the right choices to the FINISH! line where they will find Jesus.

THOUGHT TREAT: Soft Step Marshmallow Feet. Toothpick together two large marshmallows, adding five small marshmallows for toes--inserting toes into large marshmallow with toothpicks. Be careful to collect six toothpicks from each child after they have eaten--for safe disposal. To assure safety of child, use flat toothpicks.

*Primary 2-CTR A manual is published by The Church of Jesus Christ of Latter-day Saints, Salt Lake City, Utah.

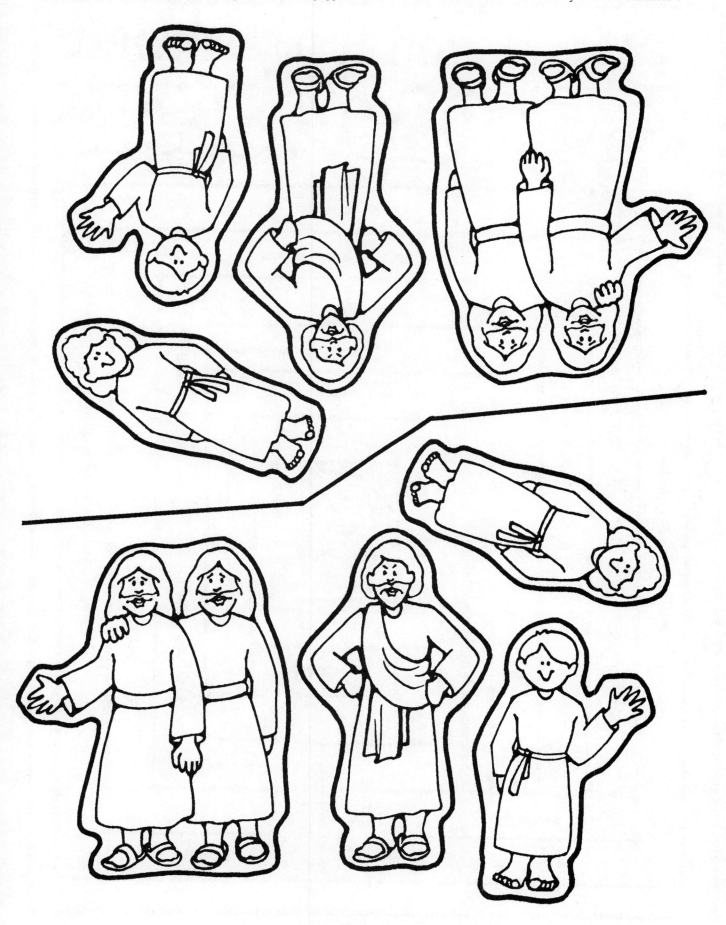

I am happy when I FOLLOW JESUS

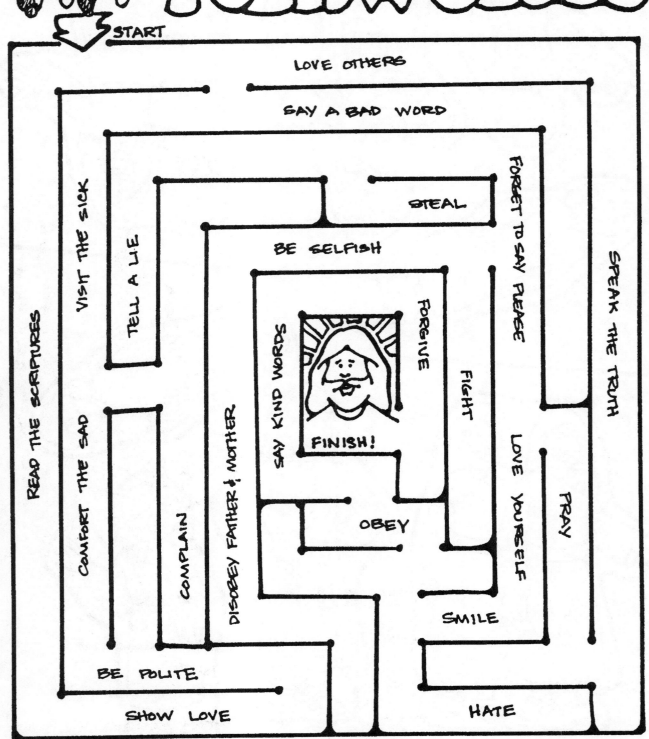

START

LOVE OTHERS

SAY A BAD WORD

STEAL

BE SELFISH

FORGET TO SAY PLEASE

SPEAK THE TRUTH

VISIT THE SICK

TELL A LIE

READ THE SCRIPTURES

COMFORT THE SAD

COMPLAIN

DISOBEY FATHER & MOTHER

SAY KIND WORDS

FORGIVE

FIGHT

LOVE YOURSELF

PRAY

FINISH!

OBEY

SMILE

BE POLITE

SHOW LOVE

HATE

GRATITUDE: I Can Give Thanks

(Gratitude Gopher's grab bag game)   See lesson #24 in Primary 2-CTR A manual*.

YOU'LL NEED: Copy of grab bag label and gratitude squares (page 34) on colored cardstock paper, a small paper lunch sack or zip-close plastic bag for each child, scissors, glue, and crayons

ACTIVITY: Help children express thanks to their Heavenly Father by looking inside the grab bag to find a gratitude square showing things they are grateful for.
1. Color and cut out grab bag label and gratitude squares.
2. Paste grab bag label on small paper lunch sack or slip inside a zip-close plastic bag (to hold gratitude squares).
3. Place squares inside bag and play the **GRATITUDE GOPHER'S GRAB BAG GAME:** Divide children into two teams on two sides of the room. Take turns, one child at a time, reaching into the bag and pulling out a gratitude square. As a child pulls out a gopher square have him or her tell one thing he or she is grateful for.
TO WIN: Gratitude squares are worth one point and gopher squares are worth five points. The team with the most points wins!

THOUGHT TREAT: Gopher Graham Crackers. Chocolate covered marshmallow cookies with white frosted teeth. Tell children that when they show gratitude like Grateful Gopher, they feel happy (point at Gratitude Gopher's big, toothy smile).

HAPPINESS: Comes From Choosing the Right

(CTR happiness wheel)   See lesson #1 in Primary 2-CTR A manual*.

YOU'LL NEED: Copy of CTR happiness wheel parts A and B (pages 35-36) on colored cardstock paper, a metal or button brad for each child, scissors, and crayons

ACTIVITY: Create a CTR happiness wheel to show that happiness comes from choosing the right. As child spins the wheel, talk about ways they can choose the right and how these choices can help them to be happy.
1. Color and cut out happiness wheels.
2. Attach part A on top of part B with a metal brad or button brad (placed in center).

TO MAKE BUTTON BRAD: Sew two buttons together on opposite sides (passing thread through the same hole) to attach window wheels.

THOUGHT TREAT: CTR Cookies. Decorate sugar cookie with frosting and write CTR with contrasting colored frosting. NOTE: Make enough for next week's lesson #2*.

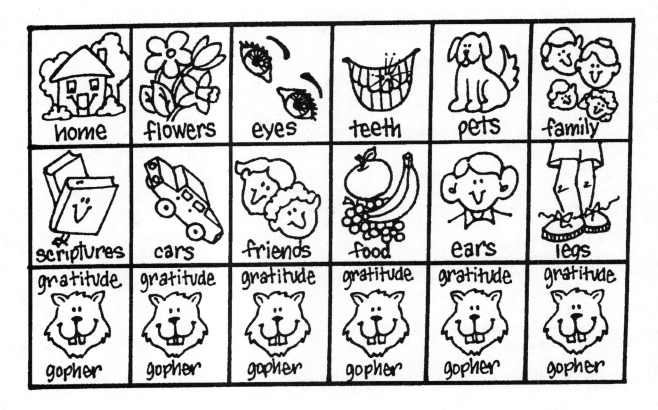

*Primary 2-CTR A manual is published by The Church of Jesus Christ of Latter-day Saints, Salt Lake City, Utah.

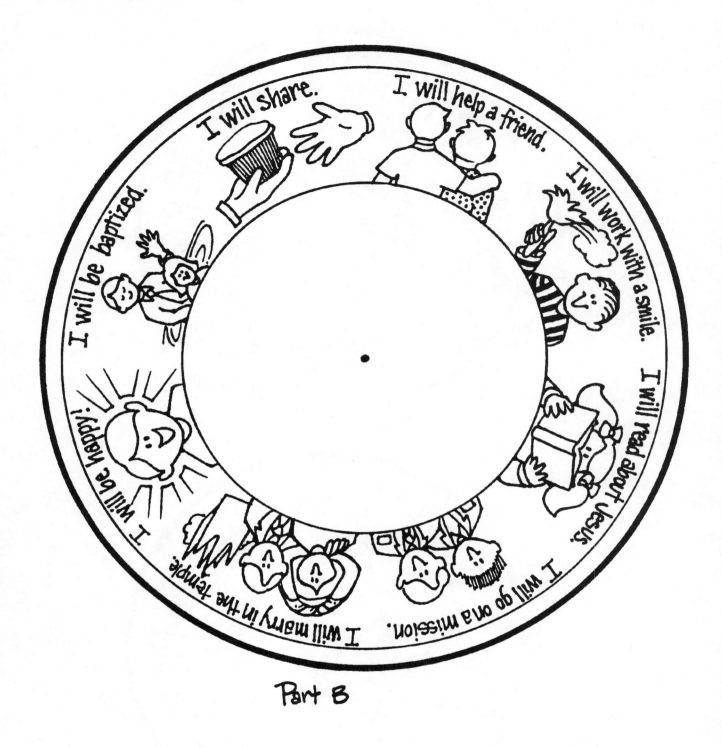

Part B

HOLY GHOST: After I Am Baptized I Receive this Gift

(Holy Ghost stand-up card)

See lesson #13 in Primary 2-CTR A manual*.

YOU'LL NEED: Copy of stand-up card (page 38) on colored cardstock paper for each child, scissors, X-ACTO® knife, or razor blade, and crayons

ACTIVITY: Create a Holy Ghost stand-up card to remind each child that after they are baptized they can receive this special gift to help them. Stand-up card reads: "The Holy Ghost speaks to my heart and to my mind."
1. Before activity, cut dotted lines with an X-ACTO® knife or razor blade.
2. Color and cut out stand-up card.
3. Fold where indicated and stand card.

THOUGHT TREAT: Heart Shaped Treats. Cookies with heart shaped candies on top, or heart shaped candies. Talk about how the Holy Ghost dwells in your heart and mind.

JESUS Is the Good Shepherd

(Find the Lost Lamb hidden picture poster)

See lesson #23 in Primary 2-CTR A manual*.

YOU'LL NEED: Copy of poster (page 39) on colored cardstock paper for each child, scissors, and crayons

ACTIVITY: Tell children to be a good shepherd and find the lost lamb ... wearing tennis shoes, a neck tie, baseball hat, bell, bow tie, and more. Color each lost lamb as soon as you (ewe) find him.

THOUGHT TREATS
Idea #1: Corral Crackers. Make a corral or fence out of graham cracker sections, gluing the corral/fence together with frosting, then eat the corral. Corral holds in the little lambs who may run away and get lost.
Idea #2: Marshmallow Lambs. Use a flat (not sharp) toothpick to place a large marshmallow on top of another large marshmallow (halfway over edge) for body and the head, using four toothpicks for the legs. Dot on eyes with frosting or melted chocolate.

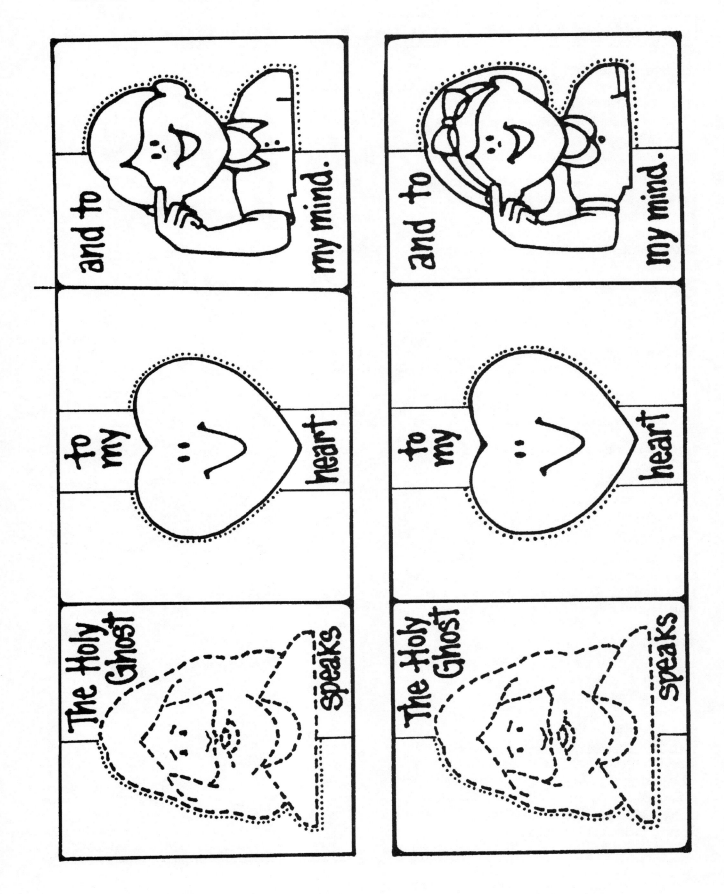

FIND THE LITTLE LOST LAMB

Find the little lost lamb ....
- wearing tennis shoes
- wearing a necktie
- wearing a baseball hat
- wearing a bell
- that is blind
- that is black
- wearing a bow tie
- wearing earrings
- wearing shorts
- wearing a belt
- with a big smile
- wearing glasses
- without ears
- with bow in wool

KINDNESS: I Can Be Kind to Others

(bite-size memorize poster - John 15:12)

See lesson #28 in Primary 2-CTR A manual*.

YOU'LL NEED: Copy of bite-size memorize poster (page 41) for each child, scissors, and crayons

ACTIVITY: To remind child that Jesus wants us to be kind to others, enjoy this bite-size memorize poster.
1. Color poster.
2. Memorize together John 15:12.

THOUGHT TREAT: <u>Give Away Goodies</u>. Make a special treat to give to someone, i.e. the bishop or neighbor, to show kindness.

KINDNESS: I Can Show Love to Every Living Creature

(I'm a Serv"ant" goggles)

See lesson #44 in Primary 2-CTR A manual*.

YOU'LL NEED: Copy of serv"ant" goggles (page 42) on colored cardstock paper and two 10" pieces of yarn or elastic for each child, scissors, paper punch, and crayons

ACTIVITY: Help children create serv"ant" goggles to wear when they show kindness to every living creature.
1. Color and cut out goggles.
2. Paper punch holes on sides.
3. Attach yarn or elastic to holes in sides to attach goggles to child's head.

THOUGHT TREAT: <u>Ants on a Log</u>. Cut celery stalks into 3" logs, fill with peanut butter and top with raisins--to resemble ants.

John 15:12

See lesson #44 in Primary 2-CTR A manual*.

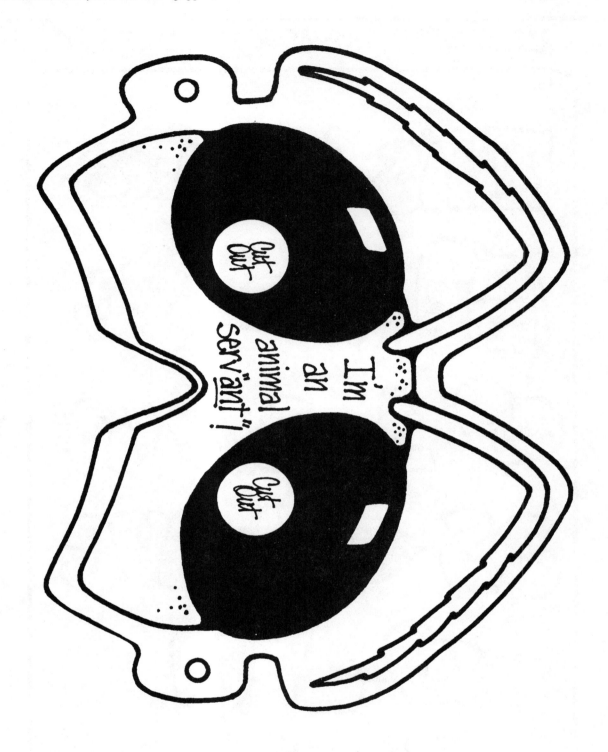

LAWS: I Believe in Obeying the Law

(law obedience badge)

See lesson #31 in Primary 2-CTR A manual*.

YOU'LL NEED: Copy of badge (page 44) on colored cardstock paper and a safety pin for each child, scissors, and crayons

ACTIVITY: Create a law obedience badge for each child to remind them to respect and obey the laws of the land.
1. Color and cut out obedience badge.
2. Safety pin badge on child's clothing.
3. Talk about raising their right hand to make a promise. Have children do this and say, "I promise to obey the laws."

THOUGHT TREAT: Five Olives on Five Fingers. Ask children to name five rules in their family to keep them safe and happy, i.e., picking up toys so others don't fall on them, putting away their clothes so they will know where they are, waiting for their turn at doing something so everyone will have a turn and no one will feel left out.

LOVE: Jesus Loves Me

(mirror message poster)

See lesson #19 in Primary 2-CTR A manual*.

YOU'LL NEED: Copy of mirror message poster (page 45) on colored cardstock paper for each child, scissors, and crayons

ACTIVITY: Create a mirror message poster children can post in the mirror to see their image next to the words: "Jesus loves Me!"
1. Cut out heart inside poster.
2. Child takes poster home to place on mirror, to see their own faces through the loving message.

THOUGHT TREAT: Heart Cut-out Sandwich and Heart Miniature Sandwiches. Make a sandwich and cut the center out to resemble poster, or let them eat the miniature cut-out heart.

*Primary 2-CTR A manual is published by The Church of Jesus Christ of Latter-day Saints, Salt Lake City, Utah.

PATTERN: LAWS (law obedience badge)   See lesson #31 in Primary 2-CTR A manual*.

44

Jesus loves

Cut out inside of heart and tape to mirror.

ME!

LOVE OTHERS: I Can Show Love By Helping

(I Love You pop-up card)

See lesson #32 in Primary 2-CTR A manual*.

YOU'LL NEED: Copy of pop-up card (page 47) on colored cardstock paper for each child, scissors, and crayons

ACTIVITY: Create a heart "I Love You" pop-up card to show a loved one you care. Encourage each child, as they give the card to someone they love, to ask that person what they can do to help.
1. Color and cut out pop-up card.
2. Fold down center of heart and cut on dotted line.
3. Fold bottom lines of heart so heart leans out.
4. Fold between A and B. Spread glue on back side of B and glue to A.

THOUGHT TREAT: Heart-to-Heart Biscuit. Make baking powder biscuits, roll out and cut out two heart-shaped biscuits for each child, laying 1/2 of the heart over the other. When sharing this heart-warming treat, tell children that when they show love to another by helping, they warm two hearts.

MISSIONARY: I Will Tell Others About Jesus Christ

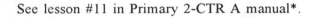

(Ammon the Missionary script-ure scene)

See lesson #11 in Primary 2-CTR A manual*.

YOU'LL NEED: Copy of Ammon, King Lamoni, Lamanites, and sheep triangle scene (pages 48-49) on colored cardstock paper for each child, scissors, glue, and crayons

ACTIVITY: Act out the story or script found in the script-ure Alma 17:17-25, using the triangle mini-scenes to show how Ammon was a missionary. Begin by saying Ammon was a great servant and a great missionary. Talk about how we can be a missionary today by serving others.
1. Color and cut out triangle scenes.
2. Fold and glue where indicated.

THOUGHT TREAT: Tracting Trail Mix. Healthy fruits, cereal, seeds, and nuts make a quick snack for Ammon as he tends King Lamoni's sheep, or for today's missionary going door to door tracting. As you eat, talk about how you could tell others about Jesus Christ.

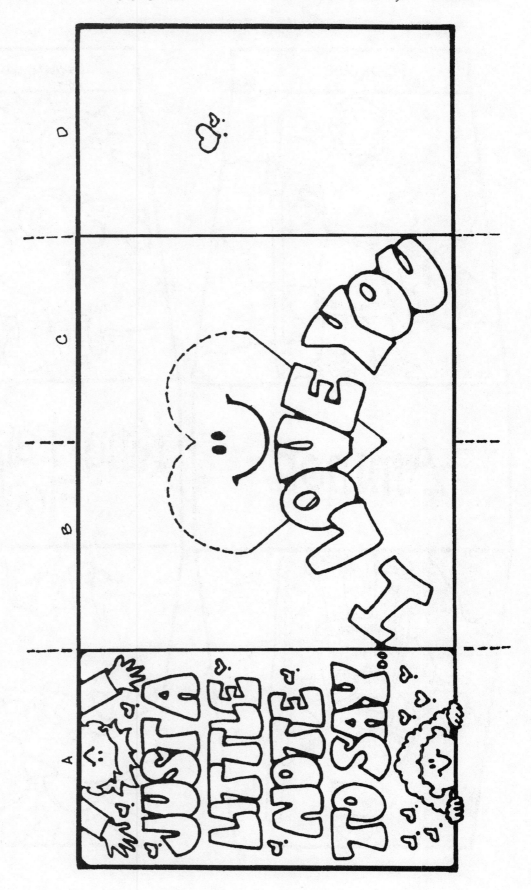

 *Primary 2 CTR-A manual is published by The Church of Jesus Christ of Latter-day Saints, Salt Lake City, Utah.

PATTERN: MISSIONARY (Ammon the Missionary script-ure scene) See lesson #11 in Primary 2-CTR A manual*.

OBEDIENCE: I Can Follow Jesus and Obey

(heavenly treasure hunt)   See lesson #30 in Primary 2-CTR A manual*.

YOU'LL NEED: Copy of treasure hunt bag label and obedience reminder cards (page 51) on colored paper and a lunch sack or a small zip-close plastic bag for each child, scissors, glue, and crayons

ACTIVITY: Have a treasure hunt to find a treasure bag filled with treats and obedience reminder cards to remind each child to be obedient and follow Jesus. This way they can receive the greatest treasure, to live with Heavenly Father again.
1. Color and cut out treasure bag label and cards.
2. Glue label to the back of a lunch sack or slip inside a zip-close plastic bag for each child.
3. Place treats and obedience reminder cards inside bag.
TREASURE HUNT: Set up treasure clues ahead of time on chairs and on wall, or give the children directions as follows (starting children in a line at the front of the room facing their chairs--have heavenly treasure bag taped to the bottom of chairs): 1) Go to your chair, don't sit down. 2) Look under chair. 3) Sit down on chair and stand up. 4) Turn three times. 5) Clap five times. 6) Smile 7) Say, "If I obey and follow the Savior, I can live with Heavenly Father. This to me is the greatest treasure." 8) Look under your chair to find a special treasure. 9) Enjoy treats.

THOUGHT TREAT: Treasure Hunt Treats. Place small candy treats inside heavenly treasure hunt bag. Remind children that candy is sweet and fun to eat, but it doesn't last long. The sweetest treasure can last and last forever. That treasure is to live with Heavenly Father. Read the sack label with children to learn the message.

PEACEMAKER: I Can Shine Bright

(I Can Shine Bright ... I'm a Peacemaker lightswitch cover)   See lesson #22 in Primary 2-CTR A manual*.

YOU'LL NEED: Copy of peacemaker lightswitch cover (page 52) on bright yellow colored cardstock paper for each child, scissors, and crayons.
OPTION: Make ahead, and cut out center of lightswitch with a razor blade.
ACTIVITY: Create a lightswitch cover children can take home and place over their lightswitch to remind them to shine bright each day, showing love and concern for others. Remind them they can make their home more peaceful by doing kind deeds and helping those in need.
1. Color and cut out lightswitch cover.
2. Place cover over a lightswitch to show how to display it in their room.

THOUGHT TREAT: Peaceful Pudding. Serve a large bowl or individual cups of pudding with a whipped creme letter "P" on top to remind children that peace starts with the letter "P." Talk of ways they can be a peacemaker, i.e., sharing toys, waiting for their turn at the drinking fountain, raising their hand before they speak in class.

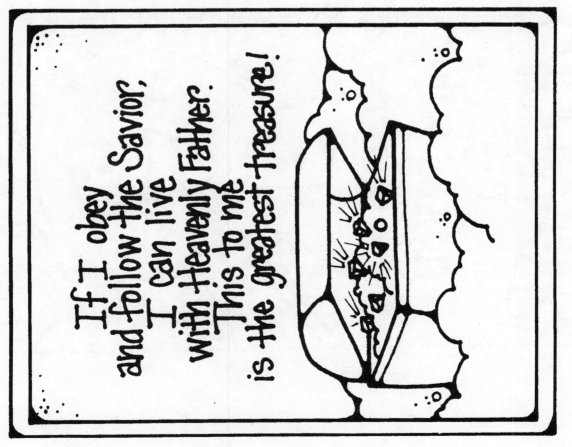

     *Primary 2-CTR A manual is published by The Church of Jesus Christ of Latter-day Saints, Salt Lake City, Utah.

PRAYER: I Can Grow Closer to Heavenly Father

(prayer rock reminder)

See lesson #10 in Primary 2-CTR A manual*.

YOU'LL NEED: Copy of prayer rock reminder (page 54) on colored cardstock paper, a small rock, and a zip-close plastic bag for each child, scissors, and crayons

ACTIVITY: Create a prayer rock reminder note to place inside a bag with a rock to remind children to pray.
1. Color and cut out Prayer Rock Reminder.
2. Place reminder in zip-close plastic bag with a rock.
3. Read reminder and role-play how to pray.

THOUGHT TREAT: <u>Heart Shaped Cookies or Sugar Cookies With Heart Candies</u>. Remind children that Heavenly Father will give them a warm, peaceful feeling in their hearts when they pray.

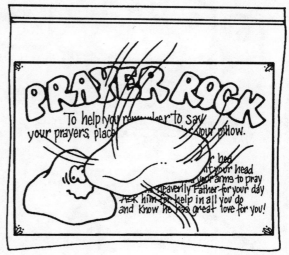

PRAYERS: Heavenly Father Hears and Answers My Prayers

("YES," "NO" wristbands)

See lesson #18 in Primary 2-CTR A manual*.

YOU'LL NEED: Copy of "YES" and "NO" wristband patterns (page 55) on colored cardstock paper and two 1/2" pieces sticky-back Velcro or tape for each child, scissors, and crayons

ACTIVITY: Create "YES" and "NO" wristbands children can wear on each wrist to help them make decisions that are best. This will help them judge how Heavenly Father might answer their prayer. The "YES" wristband reads: "YES because it's OK," and the "NO" wristband reads: "NO because it is best for me." ♥ **SITUATIONS TO DISCUSS:** The lesson* suggests several parent and child situations where children pretend to be the parent. They decide what is best for their children. Here are a few more situations.

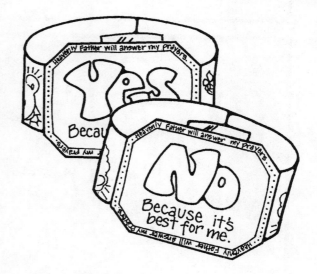

1. Your child wants his dinner, but the dog is hungry too. Do you feed him his dinner first? "NO." Why do you say that?
2. Your child wants to run out on the icy, slippery porch. Do you let him? "NO." Why do you say that?
3. The work is done and it's time for fun. Do you go to the park? "YES." Why did you say that?
4. Your child needs his sleep and it's time to go to bed. He still wants to play. "NO." Why do you say that?
5. The fish tank is dirty. Do you let your fish swim in dirty water? "NO." Why do you say that?
6. Aunt Nedra is sick and needs some loving care. Do you leave? "NO." Why did you say that?
7. Your child's favorite TV show is on, and he has helped you set the table for dinner. Do you let him watch TV? "YES." Why did you say that?

♥ **HOW TO VOTE:** Tell children they must listen carefully and only say "YES" or "NO" to the answers. When they hear "YES" they are to raise their "YES" wristband. When they hear "NO" they raise their "NO" wristband.

THOUGHT TREAT: <u>"YES" and "NO" Cookies</u> with a frosted "Y" on one and "N" on the other. Or, serve saltine crackers with "Y" or "N" written with processed cheese from the tube or can.

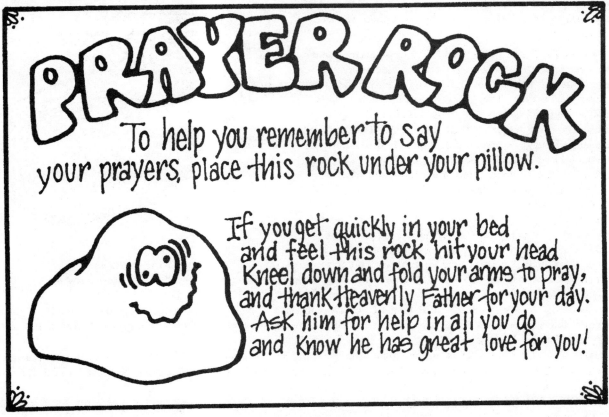

PATTERN: PRAYERS ("YES," "NO" wristbands)   See lesson #18 in Primary 2-CTR A manual*.

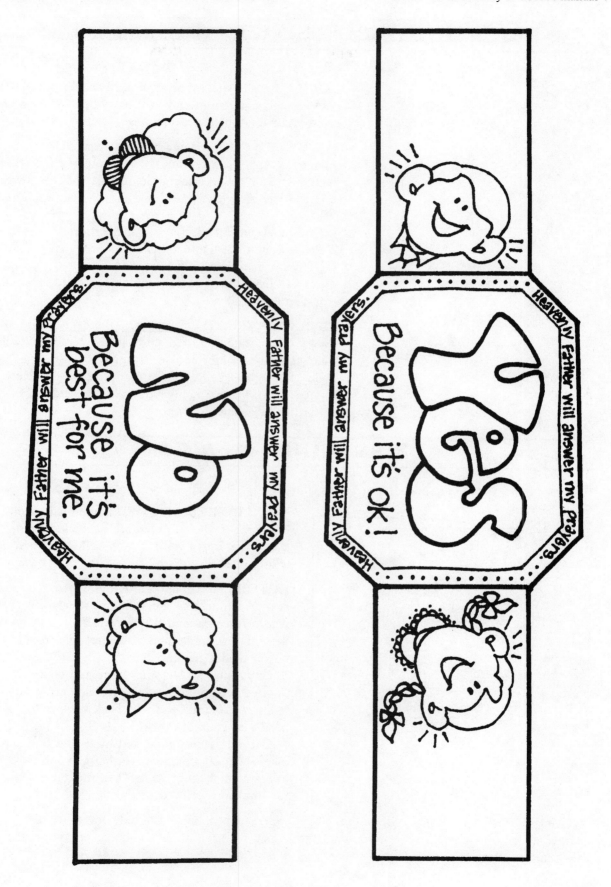

PRIESTHOOD BLESSINGS: The Priesthood Heals

(band-aid bandelo)

See lesson #16 in Primary 2-CTR A manual*.

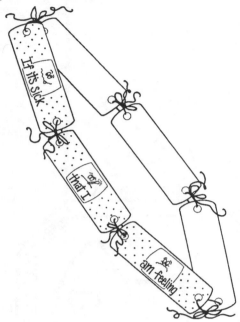

YOU'LL NEED: Copy of band-aid bandelo (page 57) on colored cardstock paper and yarn or ribbon for each child, scissors, paper punch, and crayons

ACTIVITY: Create a huge bandelo that reads:
"If it's sick that I am feeling, I'll let the priesthood do the healing." Tell children that Jesus Christ has the power to heal and has given the priesthood to us to help heal the sick.
1. Color and cut out band-aid bandelo strips.
2. Paper punch holes at each end.
3. Tie yarn or ribbon to connect ends.
4. Place a band-aid bandelo around each child's shoulder to cross over the chest.

THOUGHT TREAT: Choice #1: Bandage Shape Wafer Cookie. Decorate a frosted smile in the center of each bandage shaped wafer cookie. Choice #2: Smarties® or Candy-like Pills. Tell children that pills are not candy. Choice #3: Bandage Sandwiches. Make sandwiches and cut bread into bandage-width strips.

PRIESTHOOD Can Help Me

(Priesthood Power Calmed Seas moving ship scene)

See lesson #17 in Primary 2-CTR A manual*.

YOU'LL NEED: Copy of moving ship scene and boat (pages 58-59) on colored cardstock paper and a wooden craft stick for each child, scissors, tape, and crayons

ACTIVITY: Create a moving ship scene to remind children of the scripture in Mark 4:39 where Jesus calmed the storm. This is to remind them that Jesus helps and blesses us through the power of the priesthood.
1. Color and cut out ship scene and boat.
2. Glue boat on half of the wooden craft stick.
3. Cut out handle and fold back tabs. Glue or tape handle to back of scene.
4. Cut hole where indicated by dotted line and insert boat on stick. Move the boat back and forth to simulate a rough sea. Then move more slowly to simulate a calm sea.

THOUGHT TREAT: Banana Boat with Cheese Sails. Cut a banana in half crosswise and lengthwise and insert a slice of cheese with a toothpick for the sail. As you eat, talk about the story from Mark 4:35-41.

*Primary 2-CTR A manual is published by The Church of Jesus Christ of Latter-day Saints, Salt Lake City, Utah.

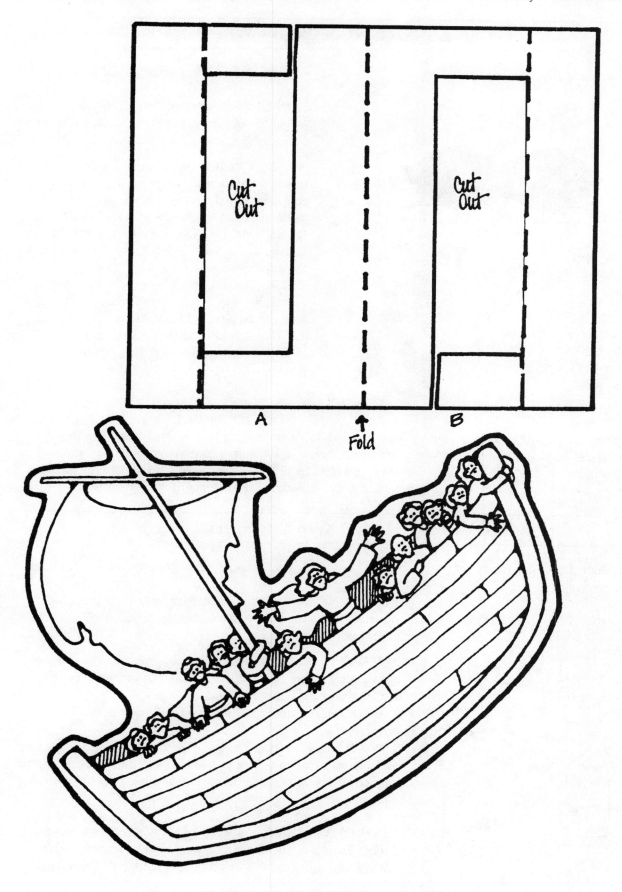

Cut Out

Cut Out

A

↑
Fold

B

*Primary 2-CTR A manual is published by The Church of Jesus Christ of Latter-day Saints, Salt Lake City, Utah.

59

REVERENCE Begins With Me

(Reverence Raccoon cap)

See lesson #21 in Primary 2-CTR A manual*.

YOU'LL NEED: Copy of raccoon cap (pages 61-62) on colored cardstock paper for each child, scissors, and crayons

ACTIVITY: Create a Reverence Raccoon cap to show children they can be like Reverence Raccoon and show reverence. Just try on this cap and watch the reverent actions start.

READY ACTIONS: Folding arms for prayer, closing eyes, bowing head, and listening while the prayer is said.

TALK ABOUT the Nephite children and how they showed reverence when they were around Jesus (3 Nephi 17:11-12, 21-24).

1. Color and cut out the raccoon cap.
2. Glue or tape sides together, matching parts A-C.
3. Attach tail back to parts C and D.

THOUGHT TREAT: Raccoon "Eye" Love You Sugar Cookies. Frost round cookies with white frosting and place a black gumdrop in the center--serve two cookies each to complete the face. Talk about raccoons and how they are so eager to be clean, washing their food before they eat it. Say, "I'll bet they even fold their arms and bow their head when a prayer is said." Reverence Raccoon says, "Reverence Begins with Me!"

SABBATH: I Can Keep this Special Day Holy

(Sabbath Day medallion)

See lesson #37 in Primary 2-CTR A manual*.

YOU'LL NEED: Copy of medallion (page 63) on colored cardstock paper and 24" yarn or ribbon for each child, scissors, paper punch, and crayons

ACTIVITY: Create a picture message medallion to strengthen each child's desire to keep the Sabbath Day a holy day.
1. Color and cut out medallion.
2. Help children figure out message and memorize the scripture.
3. Punch holes at top left and right.
4. Tie a string at each end to hang around child's neck. Show how child can take medallion home and hang on the wall or door.

THOUGHT TREAT: Sabbath Sandwich. Make a sandwich, cut off crust and cut in fourths, then with processed cheese in a tube or can squirt an "S" on each for Sunday or Sabbath Day.

*Primary 2-CTR A manual is published by The Church of Jesus Christ of Latter-day Saints, Salt Lake City, Utah.

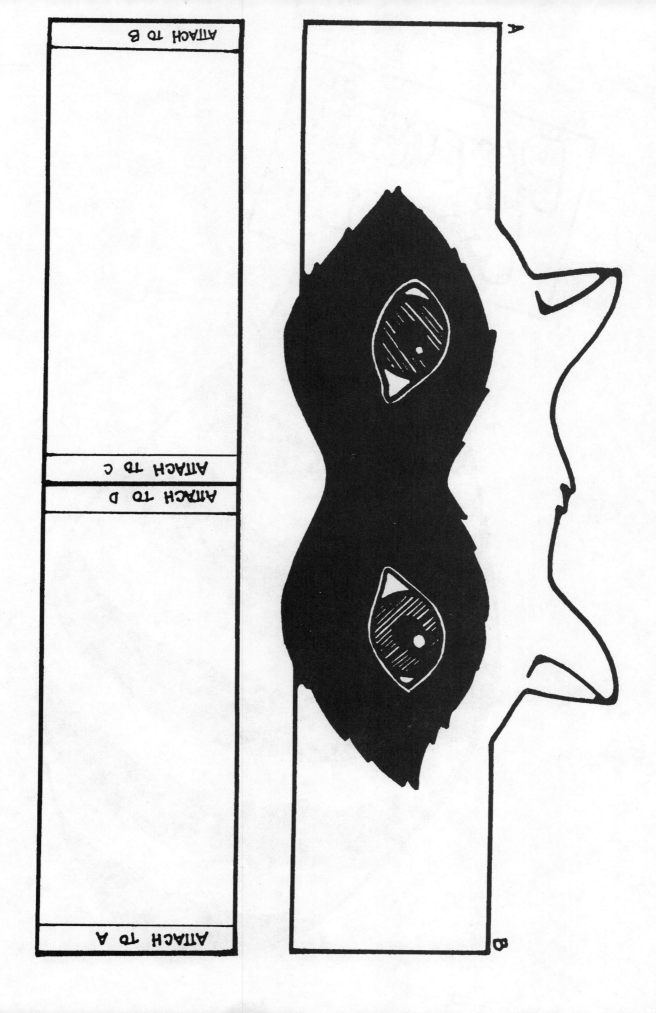

SACRAMENT: I Will Remember Jesus

(sacrament reminder bracelet)

See lesson #38 in Primary 2-CTR A manual*.

YOU'LL NEED: Copy of sacrament reminder bracelet (page 65) on cardstock paper and tape or 1/2" piece of sticky-back Velcro for each child, scissors, and crayons

ACTIVITY: Inspire a child to remember Jesus during the sacrament by looking at a bracelet that reads, "I Will Remember Jesus."
1. Color and cut out bracelet.
2. Tape or place a 1/2" piece of sticky-back Velcro on bracelet to attach to child's wrist.

THOUGHT TREAT: <u>Unleavened Bread</u>. Flat bread or pita bread to show the type of bread Jesus ate; compare it with bread that has yeast. Say, "The people ate honey with their bread." Make honey butter and serve it with bread.

SECOND COMING: I Will Be Ready When Jesus Comes Again

(two-sided medallion)

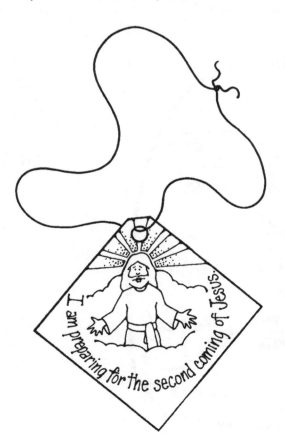

See lesson #43 in Primary 2-CTR A manual*.

YOU'LL NEED: Copy of medallion (page 66) on cardstock paper, 40" of yarn or ribbon for each child, scissors, paper punch, and crayons

ACTIVITY: Create a medallion to remind children on one side: "I Am Preparing for the Second Coming of Jesus" and on the other side "I Will Keep Heaven in Sight, as I Choose the Right." 1. Color and cut out medallion parts A and B.
2. Glue medallion back-to-back.
3. Punch a hole at the top.
4. Tie yarn or ribbon to fit around child's neck.

THOUGHT TREAT: <u>Eye Glass Cookie</u>. To see your way back to heaven. Roll sugar cookie dough and cut into 2" circles 1/4" thick. Cut a 3/4" hole in the center. Place on an aluminum foil covered baking sheet. Crush hard tack candy and fill in each cookie hole. Bake at 375° for 8-10 minutes. Hardtack candy melts into glassy appearance. Child can hold cookie to eye and pretend to see to heaven, or to look for Jesus when he comes again.

 *Primary 2-CTR A manual is published by The Church of Jesus Christ of Latter-day Saints, Salt Lake City, Utah.

PATTERN: SACRAMENT (reminder bracelet)

See lesson #38 in Primary 2-CTR A manual*.

*Primary 2-CTR A manual is published by The Church of Jesus Christ of Latter-day Saints, Salt Lake City, Utah.

PATTERN: SECOND COMING (two-sided medallion)   See lesson #43 in Primary 2-CTR A manual*.

*Primary 2-CTR A manual is published by The Church of Jesus Christ of Latter-day Saints, Salt Lake City, Utah.

SERVICE: I Can Serve Others Secretly

(secret service necklace)

See lesson #39 in Primary 2-CTR A manual*.

YOU'LL NEED: Copy of secret service hearts (page 68) on colored cardstock paper and a 26" piece of yarn or ribbon for each child, scissors, paper punch, and crayons

ACTIVITY: Have children create a secret service necklace to wear home inside their clothes to keep their planned service a secret. When they perform the secret service, they can take a heart off the necklace and leave it for the person to show that someone is serving them secretly.
1. Color and cut out secret service hearts.
2. Paper punch hearts.
3. String yarn or ribbon through hearts and tie a knot at the end to place around child's neck.

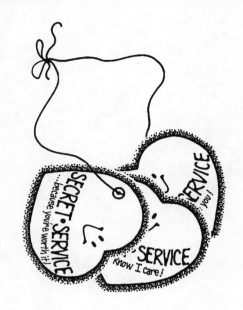

THOUGHT TREAT: Heart Shaped Treats. Tell children that each time they help another person secretly, they feel happy in their heart.

SHARING: Happy Times are Sharing Times

(treats wrapped with sharing reminders)

See lesson #27 in Primary 2-CTR A manual*.

YOU'LL NEED: Copy of treat wrappers (page 69) on lightweight paper and candy bar and/or two sticks of chewing gum for each child, scissors, tape, and crayons

ACTIVITY: Wrap up a candy bar and/or stick of gum for the child to share in class or at home. The wrapper(s) invite them to share. Since there are two sticks of gum, children could share one stick in class with a friend and take the other home to share.
1. Color and cut out candy bar and/or gum wrapper.
2. Tape wrapper(s) around candy bar and/or stick of chewing gum.
3. In class, talk about how you would share.

THOUGHT TREAT: Candy Bar or Chewing Gum to Share (see above).

PATTERN: SHARING (treat wrappers with a sharing reminder)   See lesson #27 in Primary 2-CTR A manual*.

TALENTS: Heavenly Father Gave Me Talents

(Practice Makes Purr-fect talent tally)

See lesson #35 in Primary 2-CTR A manual*.

YOU'LL NEED: Copy of cat walk talent tally and cat (page 71) on colored cardstock paper and 15" string for each child, scissors, paper punch, and crayons

ACTIVITY: To remind each child each day of a talent they can practice, create a Monday-through-Sunday cat walk, moving cat along on a string each day to remind them that "Practice Makes Purr-fect." Each time they try something, it gets easier and easier. Soon they will purr with delight that they have developed a talent, such as drawing, painting, creating something, playing an instrument, cleaning up their room, or taking care of their pets. etc.

TO MAKE TALENT TALLY:
1. Cut out tally card and cat.
2. Poke a hole in the left and right side on the "X".
3. Run string through both holes and tie in front so there is no lag in string.
4. Tape cat over knot and see how it moves back and forth.

THOUGHT TREAT: Purr-fect Bread. Make bread dough into the shape of a cat and bake at 375° for 10-15 minutes. Thread three black threads through cat's mouth with a needle and clip ends. As children eat the cat-shaped bread roll pull out one thread at a time and name three talents they want to purr-fect.

TEACHING TREASURES: I Want to Learn More About Jesus

(scripture treasure bookmark)

See lesson #20 in Primary 2-CTR A manual*.

YOU'LL NEED: Copy of scripture treasure bookmark (page 72) on colored cardstock paper for each child, scissors, paper punch, yarn, and crayons

ACTIVITY: Create a scripture treasure bookmark to help children know that the scriptures are teachings to treasure.
1. Color and cut bookmark.
2. Punch dots around border.
3. Weave yarn through holes and tie a bow at the top.
4. Read the bookmark, "The teachings of Jesus are a great treasure!"
5. Help children look up and read a scripture, John 13:17 (happy are they if they know the scriptures).

THOUGHT TREAT: Scripture Wafers. Select four wafer type cookies in the shape of scriptures. As you eat each cracker, name the scriptures: Bible, Book of Mormon, Pearl of Great Price, Doctrine and Covenants.

*Primary 2-CTR A manual is published by The Church of Jesus Christ of Latter-day Saints, Salt Lake City, Utah.

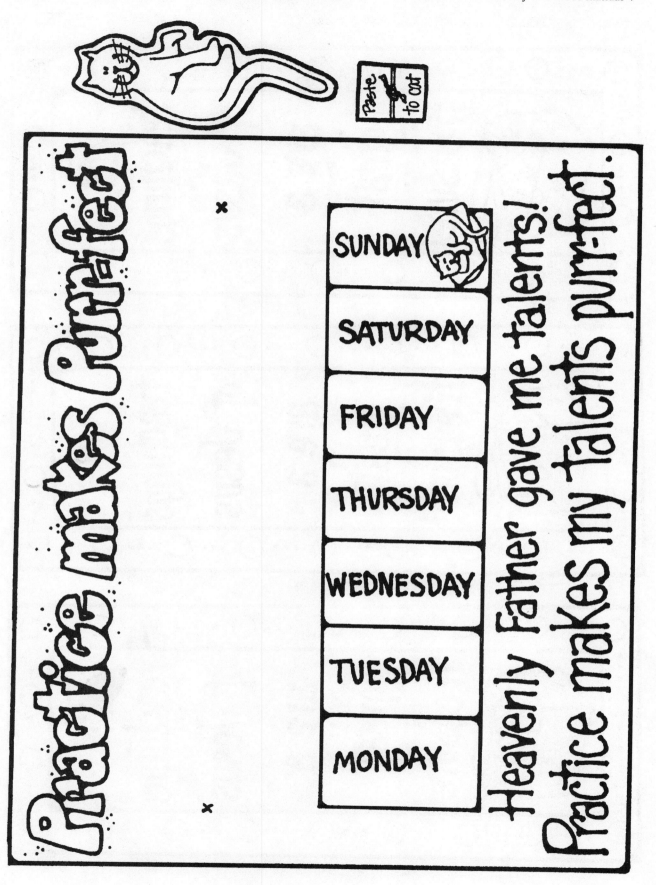

Practice makes Purr-fect

SUNDAY
SATURDAY
FRIDAY
THURSDAY
WEDNESDAY
TUESDAY
MONDAY

Heavenly Father gave me talents!
Practice makes my talents purr-fect.

Paste to cat

PATTERN: TALENTS (Practice Makes Purr-fect talent tally)   See lesson #35 in Primary 2-CTR A manual*.

PATTERN: TREASURED TEACHINGS (scripture bookmark)   See lesson #20 in Primary 2-CTR A manual*.

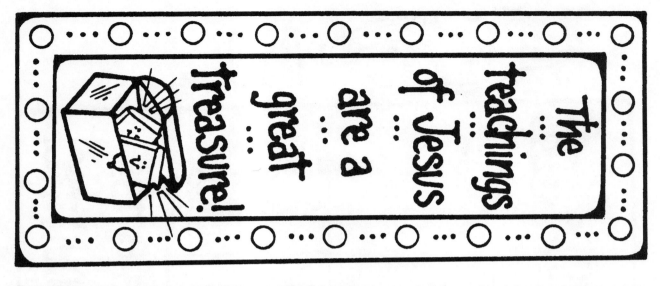

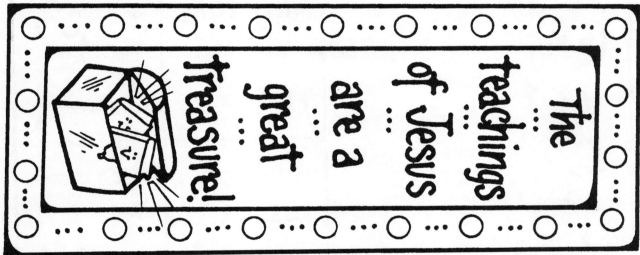

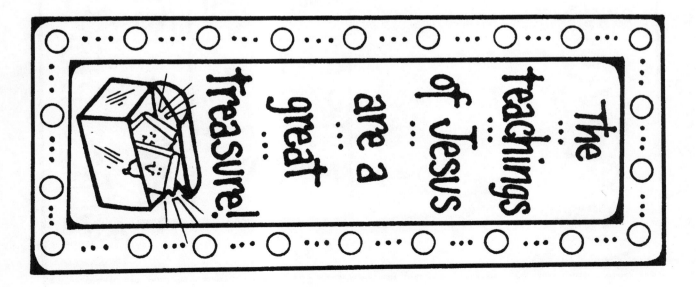

 *Primary 2-CTR A manual is published by The Church of Jesus Christ of Latter-day Saints, Salt Lake City, Utah.

TEMPTATIONS: Dare to Choose the Right

(CTR wristbands)

See lesson #14 in Primary 2-CTR A manual*.

YOU'LL NEED: Copy of CTR wristbands (page 74) on colored cardstock paper and 1" piece of sticky-back Velcro or tape for each child, scissors, and crayons

ACTIVITY: Create a wristband favor to show ways children can dare to choose the right to keep heaven in sight.
1. Color and cut out wristband favors for each child.
2. Attach sticky-back Velcro or tape to make wristband easy to put on and take off.

THOUGHT TREAT: <u>CTR Cupcakes</u>. Before baking cupcakes, write "Dare to CTR" on slips of paper, wrap in foil, and bake inside cupcake. Surprise! Children find the special reminder message.

THANK YOU: I Will Say Two Special Words

(courtesy "Thank You" card)

See lesson #25 in Primary 2-CTR A manual*.

YOU'LL NEED: Copy of courtesy card (page 75) on colored cardstock paper for each child, scissors, glue, and crayons

ACTIVITY: Help child learn to say thank you with a little note of appreciation to those who help him/her each week in church.
1. Color and cut out card.
2. Fan fold and glue front flap to middle.
3. Sign and deliver.
Card could be sent to mom or dad, bishop, chorister, special teacher, or friend.

THOUGHT TREAT: <u>Tiny Thankful Foods</u>. Finger foods children are thankful for, i.e. tiny crackers, raisins, marshmallows, carrot or apple slices. Before they eat, they must say "thank you" for every item.

When temptations come...
Say NO and... RUN!
RUN! RUN! RUN!
RUN! RUN! RUN!

DARE to be true!
DARE to do right!

 *Primary 2-CTR A manual is published by The Church of Jesus Christ of Latter-day Saints, Salt Lake City, Utah.

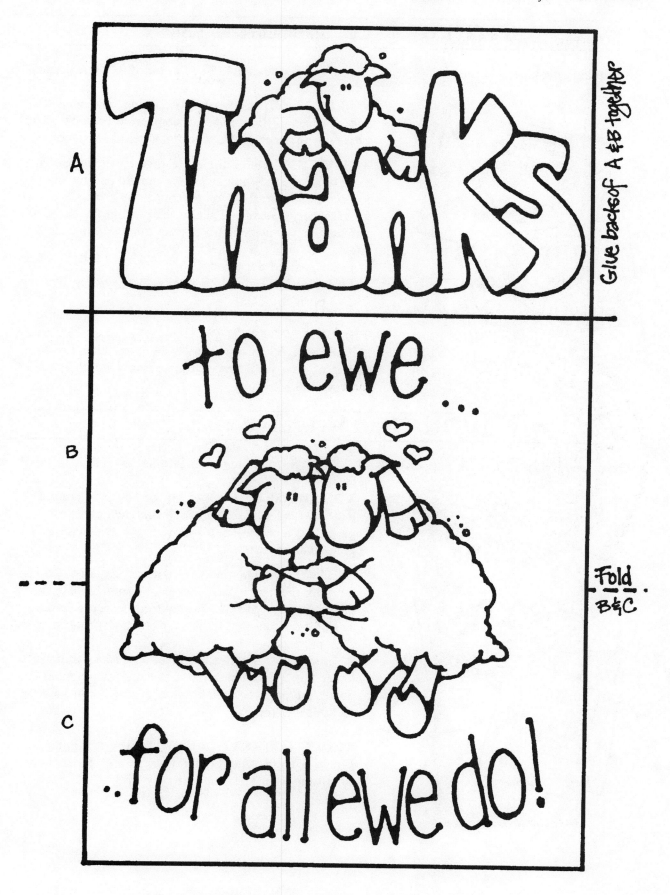

TITHING: I Can Show Love As I Share

(my tithing envelope)

See lesson #33 in Primary 2-CTR A manual*.

YOU'LL NEED: Copy of "My Tithing" envelope pattern (page 77) and tithing receipt from bishop's office (optional) for each child, scissors, glue, and crayons

ACTIVITY: Create a tithing storage envelope for each child to store ready-to-pay tithing money and receipt forms. Explain that as we pay our tithing, we show love for Heavenly Father and Jesus. Help child fill out a sample tithing envelope, to put the tithing amount in later.
1. Color and cut out envelope.
2. Fold edges and glue like an envelope, leaving top flap free to open and close.

THOUGHT TREAT: <u>Ten Bite-size Cookies</u>. Help children give one away to the bishop, explaining to the bishop of your ward that you are helping the children share 1/10th.

TRUTH: I Will Tell the Truth

(Trevor and Trina Truth sack puppets)

See lesson #34 in Primary 2-CTR A manual*.

YOU'LL NEED: Copy of girl or boy sack puppet patterns (pages 78-79) on flesh or peach cardstock paper and a small lunch sack for each child, scissors, glue, and crayons

ACTIVITY: Sometimes it's not easy to tell the truth, but with their very own Trevor or Trina Truth sack puppets, children can role-play truth-telling situations.
1. Color and cut out Trevor for boy and Trina for girl sack puppets.
2. Glue girl or boy head to bottom of sack, and chin up under flap. When children move sack flap up and down, the puppet's mouth opens to say "I can be strong and tell the truth."

THOUGHT TREAT: <u>I Chews to Tell the Truth Chewing Gum</u>. As children chew, watch mouths open to tell the truth.

*Primary 2-CTR A manual is published by The Church of Jesus Christ of Latter-day Saints, Salt Lake City, Utah.

PATTERN: TITHING (my tithing envelope)

See lesson #33 in Primary 2-CTR A manual*.

I can be strong and tell the truth!

Trevor Truth

*Primary 2-CTR A manual is published by The Church of Jesus Christ of Latter-day Saints, Salt Lake City, Utah.

PATTERN: TRUTH (Trina Truth sack puppets)   See lesson #34 in Primary 2-CTR A manual*.

I can be strong and tell the truth!

Trina Truth

Reverence Raccoon Chart

Name: _____

8	16	24	32	40	
7	15	23	31	39	46
6	14	22	30	38	45
5	13	21	29	37	44
4	12	20	28	36	43
3	11	19	27	35	42
2	10	18	26	34	41
1	9	17	25	33	

PATTERN: REVERENCE (Reverence Racoon glue-on stickers for good behavior)

Mary H. Ross, Author and
Jennette Guymon, Illustrator
are also creators of:

SUPER SCRIPTURE ACTIVITIES:
□ New Testament--I'm Trying to Be Like Jesus
□ New Testament--Tell Me the Stories of Jesus
□ New Testament--Jesus Is My Friend

PRIMARY PARTNERS:
A-Z Activities to Make Learning Fun for:
□ Nursery and Age 3 (Sunbeams)
□ CTR Ages 4-7
□ Valiant Ages 8-11

Activity books are detailed on the following pages.

MARY H. ROSS, Author

Mary Ross is an energetic mother, Primary teacher, and Achievement Days leader who loves to help children have a good time while they learn. She is a published author and columnist who has studied acting and taught modeling and voice. Her varied interests include writing, creating activities, children's parties, and cooking. Mary and her husband, Paul, live with their daughter Jennifer in Sandy, Utah.

JENNETTE GUYMON, Illustrator

Jennette Guymon has studied graphic arts and illustration at Utah Valley State College and the University of Utah. She is currently employed with a commercial construction company. She served a mission to Japan. Jennette enjoys sports, reading, cooking, art, and freelance illustrating. Jennette lives in Salt Lake City, Utah and attends the Mount Olympus Third Ward.

- Photos by Scott Hancock, Provo, Utah

More **PRIMARY PARTNERS** for
Valiant Ages 8-11 (Book of Mormon)

How do you bring Book of Mormon heroes to life for eight- to eleven-year-olds? Children this age enjoy challenges to help them develop faith in Jesus Christ, put on the armor of God, keep baptismal covenants, and be a good example, like the heroes found in the Book of Mormon.

Read of Alma and Amulek and watch the children's desire to pray and stand for right increase. Children want to follow the prophet like Nephi as he obtained the brass plates. They know they can honor their parents like Helaman's two thousand warriors. Their testimonies increase as they learn of Abinadi the prophet and the wicked King Noah. Like Captain Moroni, they can create their own Title of Liberty. They desire to repent as they learn of Alma the Younger and the Sons of Mosiah. And the purpose of life unfolds as they read of Lehi's vision of the Tree of Life.

With appealing artwork in 46 activities, you're on your way to sharing the gospel the fun way with *Primary Partners*! Enjoy puzzles, games, crafts, mazes, and scripture scrambles to promote personal testimony. Plus, you can reward children with a glue-on sticker each week for completing a SCRIPTURE CHALLENGE CARD.

The activities are designed for Primary and family home evening. You'll find the activities A-Z and cross-referenced to a particular lesson in the Primary 4 (Book of Mormon) manual.

Try These Fun Testimony Builders:

- ♥ Book of Mormon reading chart
- ♥ Commandment Concentration game
- ♥ Honor Roll merit match
- ♥ Fight for Right! word choice
- ♥ Nephite and Lamanite peace poster
- ♥ Plug into Priesthood Power Lines
- ♥ Alma the Younger's Road to Repentance maze
- ♥ 3-D box with Tree of Life Vision
- ♥ Ship-shape family goal chart
- ♥ Faith-ful saints guessing game
- ♥ Waters of Mormon word search
- ♥ Straight and Narrow Arrow scripture ruler
- ♥ Humble deeds secret service
- ♥ Personal golden plates
- ♥ Guardian angel doorknob reminder
- ♥ Who is Abinadi? prophet poster
- ♥ Wilderness Journey object find
- ♥ Cycle of history wheel
- ♥ Prayer plaque and more ...